Your Guide to Overcoming Depression: The Silent Killer

Causes and solutions that work

for defeating a disease

that affects over

18 million Americans!

Joan Rubar

Printed in the United States of America.

ISBN 978-1-300-45013-9

Table of Contents

Definition of Depression

Depression is usually defined as a psychiatric disorder with the inability to concentrate and with additional symptoms:

- ❖ insomnia
- ❖ hopelessness
- ❖ thoughts of death (a final means of peace of mind)

It is recommended that those that feel like this should seek professional help.

Facts About Depression

Over *eighteen million* American adults are experiencing major depression. This depression can signal a serious medical illness, and medical professional care may be necessary for you to take control of this illness ... but you can begin to help yourself immediately by learning more about the possible origins, mechanisms, and treatments for depression.

Depression is an extremely complex illness. There are several reasons and causes.

- ❖ Physical Abuse, as a child or adult
- ❖ Sexual Abuse at any time of life
- ❖ Emotional Abuse

- ❖ Certain medications, like beta blockers or reserpine (used to treat blood pressure)
- ❖ Personal Conflicts with family, friends, co-workers or bosses
- ❖ Death of a family member or close friend
- ❖ Genetics. Many researchers believe there is a strong genetic component to depression, though the mechanism – the 'depression gene' – has yet to be identified
- ❖ Major Life-Changes. Even positive changes can create a high level of Major events. Even good events

such as starting a new job, graduating, or getting married can lead to depression. So can moving, losing a job or income, getting divorced, or retiring.

❖ Other personal problems. Problems such as social isolation due to other mental illnesses or being cast out of a family or social group can lead to depression.

❖ Serious illnesses. Sometimes depression co-exists with a major illness or is a reaction to the illness.

❖ Substance abuse. Nearly 30% of people with substance abuse problems also have major or clinical depression. Certain medications can cause or increase your chance of getting depressed such as blood pressure drugs-beta blockers or reserpine. We are all biologically different.

Different Kinds Of Depression

In today's society, it's becoming a common condition. Depression is an emotional state of mind and recovery can take a considerable length of time. There are several different kinds of depression. The four most well-known types:

1. **Clinical Depression** can be both a psychological and physical condition and is different from having the "blues". It impacts you on everything such as sleeping, eating, mood, thinking, ability to work, study effectively, energy levels and

more.

In major depression conditions, the following symptoms are present most of the day: constant sadness, low energy, irritability, feeling worthless or guilty for no reason, difficulty concentrating and doing minor daily tasks due to lack of desire or loss of interest in your daily activities and to sleep.

2. **Dysthymia.** This type of depression frequently starts in childhood and continues through

adulthood. They never seem to be happy or remembering it. Low mood appears to be normal for that person. This depression appears to be more in women than men. An individual will seek treatment when the illness becomes more severely dysthymic and family insists this person gets medical help.

3. **Bipolar Disorders** are different from other depressions. This type is known as "Manic Depressive Disorders". People have different mood swings, need little or no sleep.

Their speech may be rapid and go on non-stop. Episodes of these symptoms may occur years apart and goes untreated. It usually occurs early in life and treatment is recommended.

4. **Post Partum Depression** is a major depression that occurs in women after childbirth. It is thought that hormonal changes in women before and after childbirth cause this. About 10% of women are affected and usually with women who have had depression before

and after giving birth to a child.
There are many additional factors
that may contribute to this
condition.

Source: *Studies done by the Aventura Stress Relief Center, Florida.*

Different Types Of Treatments for Depression

Dr. J. Ramond DePaulo, MD, Professor of Psychiatry and a Director of the Affective Disorders Clinic at John Hopkins School of Medicine. Dr. DePaulo has a very clear understanding of depression, causes, effects and treatments. Education in dealing with this can make a huge difference and the different kind of treatment available.

For years, doctors have been recommending that patients take the common-sense approach to good health:

❖ A good night sleep

❖ A nutritious diet, eating 3 meals a day

❖ Regular exercise.

Using this approach, patients do get better … but it may take longer. Patients who are on alcohol and drugs, in Dr. DePaulo's experience, are less likely to recover, and patients should abstain from the use of these. However, the patients must be willing to abstain from the use of drugs and alcohol.

"75% of patients who abstain from the use of alcohol and drugs will recover," Dr. DePaulo states. "25% will recover within two years. Relapses do occur in some people, and recovery can vary enormously according to this study of professionals."

Self-Help for Different Kinds of Depression

A person can do several things to improve your mood without the use of medication and getting professional help.

- ❖ **Any exercise activity.** Discuss your condition with family and friends that you can confide in can be helpful.

- ❖ **Refrain from making important decisions until you feel better.**

- ❖ **Diet.** A diet can be helpful. Eat fruits and vegetables. Good carbohydrates and protein. Fish.

Avoid junk food and sugar that can

contribute to a downturn in your

improvement.

Anti-Depressants

There are problems with taking anti-depressants:

1. They fail to correct the problem-the behaviors that cause the depression and the disorder recurs.

2. Drugs may give you a change and some relief but do not rectify the disorder.

3. There can be serious side effects after taking drugs to treat an illness.

Studies show that there are no drugs that can help many people suffering with depression.

Alternative Treatments for Depression

Make the first move toward the life you deserve. Knock out depression with "natural" methods.

1. If you are on a medically prescribed diet, be sure to check with your doctor before making any changes.

2. Otherwise, focus your diet on healthy foods. The mind-body connection is a powerful one and the health of one affects the other.. Try eating low sugar, high fiber and

protein foods. Fresh fruits and vegetables, lean protein and whole grains are recommended.

3. Try supplements. A good food-based multivitamin and a calcium supplement are suggested. Fish oil helps brain function as well as other benefits. Other good supplements include:

   a) **5 HTP (hydroytryplophan)** is a supplement that assists in mood regulation. It is a natural antidepressant when taken.

b) **L-theanine, amino acid** has been extensively researched and shown to promote relaxation and not causing drowsiness, an anxiety supplement.

4. **Omega-3 diet**. Shannon Cook, personal growth expert, has written several articles on holistic personal growth, physical emotions and relationship health. He recommends fatty acids, such as, Omega-6 and Omega-3 in a ratio of 5:2. Fatty acids Omega-6 are found in pork, beef and dairy. Most

people in this country get enough of Omega-6 fatty acids but not enough Omega-3. Omega-3 fatty acids are:

a) Flax seed or flax seed oil

b) Cod liver oil

c) Cold water fish such as trout, herring, sardines, salmon and mackerel

5. **Avoid food that is fried and rich in fat.** Avoid junk food and limit beverages with caffeine.

6. **Lots of fruits and vegetables should be included daily in your diet.** You need to take responsibility for your

health in the form of nurturing your body to prevent diseases. Your health should be your priority. In order to do that, you have to eat properly.

7. **Holy basil (Tulsi tea).** This is an organic herb from India. This herb helps you to stay calm and relax. It promotes normal physiological function of the body based on the researched done by Dr. Narendra. He also states that Tulsi tea is one of the best adaptogens of all the herbs he researched. It is also rich in antioxidants. This can also be found as "holy basil" in capsules. There are

numerous other health benefits from

this product.

Serotonin and Brain Chemistry

The chemical "serotonin" calms the brain and is known as a neurotransmitter that allows communications between the brain and the body. Also, scientists have found that cortisol, a stress hormone, is found in excess in people who are depressed.

Medications are used to treat depression and must be prescribed and supervised by a medical professional.

Depleted serotonin levels in the brain, reported by "Rattle, ND," are commonly treated with (anti-depressants) drugs that do not treat the cause of depression nor fix the problem. He suggests to "try to concentrate on the moment, not the day before or tomorrow." Some physical activity, taking a walk could be helpful. Good fats, such as (Omega 3) are necessary and important in the creation of new brain cells and serotonin. Then the brain can function properly.

The Gut-Brain Connection
Statements from Dr. Mercola

Researches around the world have linked gut problems to brain disorders. Your gut and brain work in conjunction with each other. That is why your intestinal health can have a profound influence on your mental health and vice versa. As a result, it should be obvious that your diet is closely linked to your mental health, and lack of nutrition can have an adverse effect on your mood and behavior. This was based on the study done by Dr. Rochelly Diaz Heytz.

Studies indicate that getting enough "brain food" – like Omega 3 fatty acids – is key. Most people are deficient in Omega 3 fats. What's more, your overall diet is just as important.

Consider eliminating most sugar and grains, as these increase your risk of insulin resistance, which is also linked to depression. Studies indicate that excessive release of insulin could be a result of and increased release of counter-regulatory hormones linked to depression.

Sources:

Henke online January 10, 2011

New Toronto January 13-20, 2011

Alternative Treatment:
Neurostar TMS Therapy

TMS (Transcranial Magnetic Stimulation) does offer hope.

This treatment was approved by the FDA in 2008, according to the manufacturer of the TMS machine.

Statistics indicate that 1 out of 3 patients experience a complete cure of depression and 1 out of 2 showed a great improvement. (This treatment may or may not be covered by your insurance company).

The part of the brain that controls your mood and depression has been identified. It is the "left prefrontal cortex". It has been found tha this part of the brain can be made to perform properly again by shooting electromagnetic pulses to the target area of the skull.

The technology based on this technique is called Transcranial Magnetic Stimulation. There are only about fourteen centers that offer this treatment. You can locate them if you do a little research.

Alternative Treatment:
St. John's Wort

St. John's Wort, an herb, is famous worldwide for supporting emotional health and well-being, and believed to help with less severe depression. Best of all, no prescription is needed.

Physicians in Germany and other countries actually prescribe St. John Wort for mild depression, especially in children and adolescents. A report from *The Cochrane Review* states:

> *The available evidence suggests that the Hypericum extracts tested in the included trials a) are superior to*

placebo in patients with major depression; b) are similarly effective as standard antidepressants; and c) have fewer side-effects than standard antidepressants.

Standardized extracts are generally available over the counter, though in some countries (such as the Republic of Ireland) a prescription is required. Extracts are usually in tablet or capsule form, and also in teabags and tinctures.

St. John's Wort may reduce the effect of drugs as well as contraceptive pills. It is known that women on contraceptive pills have become pregnant. It is recommended you consult your physician first.

Certain vitamins can affect depression as well. *The American Journal of Clinical Nutrition* reveals a "lower risk" of developing depression for people who consume greater amounts of vitamin B6 and B12. At Rush University Medical, research revealed also that higher intake of vitamins B6 and B12 from foods and supplements were associated with decreased symptoms of depression, and older adults receive positive results over time.

Alternative Treatment: Positive Thoughts

You don't have to live with depression. Try these techniques to take control of your thoughts and make an effort on your own:

- ❖ Try to think of the good things that you have in life.
- ❖ Concentrate on thoughts of your accomplishments.
- ❖ Think of positive thoughts.
- ❖ People have a tendency to keep their negative emotions and thoughts deep inside themselves, so get

involved in activities you enjoy instead of letting your mind drift back into negative thoughts.

Natural supplements are also helpful: Amino acids help support mood, sleep and energy. It may take longer to take effect when you take natural supplements.

Alternative Treatment:
Acupuncture and Massage

Dr. Jiang states that lack of harmony in the body is the cause of depression according to Chinese medicine. He suggests weekly acupuncture treatments and herbal medicine are helpful in treating depression.

Healy states "a good massage" is likely to alleviate symptoms of depression. Massage therapy has been used in China for more than 3,000 years; they believe it releases hormones that can address both physical aches and pains and the emotional as well as biochemical origins of depression.

Rubbing, stretching, and manipulating muscle mass relieves tension in muscles, increases blood flow, and promotes relaxation. Rigidity in muscles and connective tissue is not only painful, it can also limit movement and cause inflammation, which can further contribute to chemical imbalances in the body and trigger depression.

There are many different styles of massage, including:

❖ **Swedish massage** is probably the most common – a gentle method that employs smooth, circular kneading action.

- ❖ **Aromatherapy massage** combines massage with scented oils to reduce stress and generate new energy.

- ❖ **Deep tissue massage** is usually used to treat muscles that have grown tight from stress and other challenges. It focuses on the muscles and connective tissure that are closest to the bone.

- ❖ **Shiatsu** is a style that originated in Japan and uses the principle of acupuncture to focus on specific points on the body, but does not involve needles.

- ❖ **Hot stone massage** is often found in spas or massage parlors. Flat stones that have been warmed are placed on the body to promote relaxation; the therapist may also apply pressure to the stones to further relieve tension.

❖ **Reflexology** focuses on the foot, and relies on 'target lines' in the feat that are believed to correspond to specific regions and organs in the body. Many people praise reflexology as path to re-balance and new calm.

Alternative Treatment: Diet

Potatoes with skin, starchy vegetables, fresh fruit and other complex carbohydrates. In the evening, a piece of fruit before you go to bed will help your depression.

Raw materials are needed to make serotonin. Proteins provide Amino Acids and are the body's building blocks. Amino acids build muscles, bones, anti-bodies, enzymes (a complex, mostly protein products). Although we eat enough protein, it is not in balance with other food. It is recommended to eat less protein at night and more complex carbohydrates, so the body can make serotonin such

as stone ground bread and granola.

Alternative Treatment:
Amoryn

"Amoryn" is another proven herbal remedy for depression. Over thirty clinical trials has shown Amoryn relieves depression and anxiety. 87% to 90% of the people who use Amoryn show positive results.

When using this product, you need to follow directions for the recommended daily dose, and it should be taken with food. Children from 12 to 18 years of age should not take it without the supervision of a parent or guardian, and only with the approval of an alternative doctor.

As the Amoryn company says, Amoryn's main ingredient is *hyperforin*, a substance that has been clinically proven to relieve depression and decrease anxiety. By "boosting the brain's natural capacity for happiness," Amoryn restores emotional vitality without unpleasant side effects.

According to its manufacturer, after taking Amoryn for six weeks, nearly 90% of users positive results. You can also find the company's scientific research and read testimonials from real people on their web site, www.amoryn.com.

Alternative Treatment: Vitamins and Minerals

Dr. Whitaker notes that he gets good results when he treats his patients with Omega 3 fatty acids – that they work just as well as anti-depressants, with no side effects. He also found that Vitamin D, maintained at proper levels, can be helpful.

Vitamin D is an essential nutrient and "people with low levels of Vitamin D are 11 times more likely to get depression," he says. A study published in September, 2010 in an issue of the *Archives of General Psychiatry* states that Vitamin D may also reduce the incidence of schizophrenia. According to this study, you need to eat nutritional foods. They have an immense input on your mood and ability to be happy.

Mental and physical health is are equally important. It has been reported many times that drugs are rarely the answer. Dr. Whitaker states, "Natural treatments with a knowledgeable natural healthcare practitioner will help you overcome depression if you want to be happy and healthy."

Dr. James S. Gordon is a well-known expert on the importance of exercise in treating depression. He states in an interview with Dr. Mercola that physical movements can improve mood, relieve anxiety and alleviate the symptoms of depression. His recent book is *Unstruck Your Guide to the Seven Stage Journal out Of Depression.*

Drug Use for Depression by Dr. Joseph Mercola and Dr. Whitaker talks extensively about the dangers of drug use. In it, Dr. Whitaker explains the history of those with severe mental illness and the 600% increase in disabilities of psychiatric drug users.

The drug companies will not admit how dangerous these drugs can be and that they are capable of disabling-often permanently the body, brain and spirit." he says.

Dr. Whitaker, in his research, points out in his interview with Dr. Mercola, that, "in most cases, drugs cause even more serious mental disorders than the one you are being treated for." He encourages people to read these books to learn more in detail about how the "Big Pharma" companies push their drugs by giving grants and other funding to medical schools and much, much more (It is a known fact: money is behind this).

Depression in the Young

Feeling of sadness can be experienced by everyone. Sadness can linger and interfere with our daily activities.

Dr. Paul Ratle, ND, a naturopathic practitioner at Northwestern Health Sciences University's Woodwinds Natural Care Center in Woodbury, Minnesota, stated "There are a whole range of people who are mildly depressed. The question is, how much of their day is affected by it?"

We all may experience the blues from time to time but clinical depression may be the result of physical or emotional trauma. How do we know the difference between normal blues and clinical depression? If sadness is for an extended period of time, the following symptoms may be present:

- ❖ Excessive sleeping
- ❖ Appetite changes
- ❖ Weight gain

Medications or drugs can also be the cause of increase of weight. This has occurred with a family member that takes medications for depression.

Students can be particularly vulnerable to depression, and often exhibit symptoms that include loss of weight can occur, withdrawal from family, and loss of interest in studies. Making decisions may become difficult and graduating from school or college may also become a problem.

There are many complex factors contributing to depression.

Depression in the Elderly

Depression in older Americans often goes unrecognized, and is brushed off as sadness or a "natural" melancholy. Often, it is not treated properly. However, elderly depression should be taken seriously as an illness, and treated accordingly.

Symptoms and causes of depression are twice as likely to occur in women as in men. Hormonal changes in women due to puberty and other contributing factors such as menstruation, pregnancy, miscarriage and other traumas may contribute to the increased rate of depression in women.

The Importance of Melatonin

An investigation of major depression in adolescents and children found that melatonin levels were significantly lower in subjects who were clinically depressed.

There are a number of drugs that can rob your body of melatonin:

- ❖ Alcohol
- ❖ Nicotine
- ❖ Caffeine
- ❖ Sleep Aids
- ❖ NSAIDs

- ❖ Steroids

- ❖ Anti-anxiety medications

Also, low levels of melatonin can contribute to insomnia, sleep/wake disorders, OPMS. Low levels of melatonin in the elderly may be the reason why the elderly suffers from insomnia.

When scientists gain a better understanding of the causes of this illness, health professionals will be better able to diagnose and prescribe more effective treatments for depression in adults.

Conclusion

The information in this book about the many causes and many symptoms of 'depression' may help you overcome and recover from this serious malady. It may also allow you to understand and have the knowledge to help anyone you know who may be suffering from depression so they can defeat this disease and allow it to become nothing more than a forgotten memory.

You simply need to take action and be serious about defeating this illness.

References and a Reading List

Dealing with Depression Naturally: Alternatives and Complementary Therapies for Restoring Emotional Health, Syd Baumel

Gut and Psychology Syndrome: Natural Treatment for Autism, Dyspraxia, A.D.D., Dyslexia, A.D.H.D., Depression, Schizophrenia, Natasha Campbell-McBride

.Manage Stress Response, End Depression: Natural Medicine Treatment for Stress & Depression, Ronald J Fisher ND and Caryn H Wichmann ND

Healing Depression & Bipolar Disorder Without Drugs: Inspiring Stories of Restoring Mental Health Through Natural Therapies, Gracelyn Guyol

The Prozac Alternative: Natural Relief from Depression with St. John's Wort, Kava, Ginkgo, 5-HTP, Homeopathy, and Other Alternative Therapies, Ran Knishinsky

Depression-Free, Naturally: 7 Weeks to Eliminating Anxiety, Despair, Fatigue, and Anger from Your Life, Joan Mathews Larson

Depression Solutions: Therapy, Natural Treatments or Medication?, Maria C. Lloyd

Natural Medicine Guide to Bipolar Disorder, The: New Revised Edition, Stephanie Marohn

Natural Medicine Guide to Depression (The Healthy Mind Guides), Stephanie Marohn

Unstruck: Your Guide To The Seven Stage Journey Out Of Depression., Dr. Joseph Mercola

Drug Use for Depression, Dr. Joseph Mercola and Dr. Whitaker

5-HTP: The Natural Way to Overcome Depression, Obesity, and Insomnia, Michael T. Murray

Could It Be B12?: An Epidemic of Misdiagnoses, Sally M. Pacholok

Nutrition and Mental Illness: An Orthomolecular Approach to Balancing Body Chemistry, Carl Curt Pfeiffer

Natural Prozac: Learning to Release Your Body's Own Anti-Depressants, Joel C. Robertson

Rebuild from Depression: A Nutrient Guide Including Depression in Pregnancy and Postpartum, Amanda Rose Ph.D.

The Omega-3 Connection: The Groundbreaking Antidepression Diet and Brain Program, Andrew L. Stoll

Power of Vitamin D: A Vitamin D Book That Contains the Most Comprehensive and Useful Information on Vitamin D Deficiency, Vitamin D Level, Sarfraz Zaidi